LEGO® Harry Potter

WITCHES AND WIZARDS OF HOGWARTS HANDBOOK

BY SAMANTHA SWANK

SCHOLASTIC INC.

CONTENTS

INTRODU

The Wizarding World is full of magic, danger, adventure, and excitement—especially once you turn eleven! That's when young witches and wizards begin Hogwarts School of Witchcraft and Wizardry, where they learn how to cast spells, brew potions, and battle monsters that live in secret underground dungeons. Okay, that last part might not be part of the official curriculum, but it has happened at Hogwarts! And outside of Hogwarts, the excitement only continues. There are secret organizations, high-stakes battles, and undercover missions at the Ministry of Magic.

From Harry Potter—"the Boy Who Lived"—to Albus Dumbledore—the greatest headmaster Hogwarts ever had—to Salazar Slytherin, one of the school's founders and probably Voldemort's great-great (great-great-great? who knows?!) grandfather, the Wizarding World is full of heroes, villains, and everyone in between. And who could forget Harry's friends (Hermione and Ron, Luna, and Neville), his rivals (Draco Malfoy and Professor Snape), and his worst enemy (You-Know-Who)? Wait, you DO know who You-Know-Who is, right? Well, this is awkward. But don't worry—you'll learn all about him here!

CTION

FIND OUT WHICH AUROR HAS THE BEST SECRET DISGUISES AND WHO THOUGHT LIVING AS A RAT FOR TWELVE YEARS WAS STILL BETTER THAN GOING TO AZKABAN PRISON (HE MIGHT BE RIGHT). LEARN ALL THERE IS TO KNOW ABOUT SOME OF THE MOST IMPORTANT CHARACTERS IN THE WIZARDING WORLD!

HOGWARTS STUDENTS

Hogwarts School of Witchcraft and Wizardry is a school for young witches and wizards located in Great Britain. Students receive a letter inviting them to attend Hogwarts when they turn eleven years old—and unlike many young Muggles, they can't WAIT for summer vacation to end and school to begin. Hey, you would feel that way, too, if your school taught you to make objects fly or to turn a rat into a goblet. That's important stuff!

First years are sorted into one of four houses when they arrive at the castle. Gryffindor for those who are brave and daring, Slytherin for those who are cunning and ambitious, Ravenclaw for those who are intelligent and witty, and Hufflepuff for those who are loyal and hardworking.

Over the course of seven years, students learn how to brew potions, cast spells, tend to magical plants and animals, and more. At the end of each year, the students are tested on what they've learned, just like at a Muggle school. That's right—even magic won't get you out of taking exams here!

But Hogwarts isn't only for homework. Let's get to the good stuff! The houses also compete for a House Cup and a Quidditch Cup. There are student clubs and field trips to Hogsmeade village, where you can stuff your face with candy from Honeydukes Sweet Shop and then buy a Nose-Biting Teacup from Zonko's Joke Shop to play a prank on your friend—the perfect afternoon!

HARRY POTTER

YOU'D THINK FIGHTING DARK WIZARDS WOULD GET ME OUT OF TAKING TESTS, RIGHT?

ALSO KNOWN AS:

"THE BOY WHO LIVED" AND "THE CHOSEN ONE"

Harry Potter has been famous ever since he was a baby. That's when he becomes the first-ever wizard to survive the Avada Kedavra Curse, after Lord Voldemort attacks his family. Not bad for a little guy who still wears a diaper! From then on, every witch and wizard knows his name—but little Harry has no idea about the magical world that awaits him. He is raised by his Muggle relatives, the Dursleys, who are so cruel that they make Filch, the grumpy Hogwarts caretaker, seem downright jolly in comparison!

On Harry's eleventh birthday, he learns that he is a wizard. He begins school at the Hogwarts School of Witchcraft and Wizardry. But Hogwarts isn't a normal school! In between classes and homework, Harry manages to get in the middle of countless mysteries and adventures, and maybe a little trouble, too . . .

At the end of his first school year, Harry survives another encounter with Lord Voldemort when he protects the Sorcerer's Stone from being stolen. But the fight with Voldemort isn't over—that guy won't just get a hobby and leave Harry alone! Throughout his time at Hogwarts, Harry shows bravery and loyalty again and again in the battle against Voldemort and his followers.

PATRONUS:
STAG

HARRY POTTER

MY FRIENDS MAKE ME FEEL LIKE THE LUCKIEST WIZARD AROUND! EXCEPT FOR THAT VOLDEMORT-ALWAYS-OUT-TO-GET-ME THING.

Harry's time at Hogwarts isn't just fighting bad guys and learning magic. He also spends time with a great group of friends, including his BFFs, Ron and Hermione. Ron and Harry become friends right away, but it isn't until later that they become friends with Hermione, too. The three of them battle an escaped troll in the girls' bathroom, defeating it by sticking a wand up its nose and clubbing it over the head. That's one way to bond with new friends!

Ron and Hermione are always there for Harry and willing to lend a hand. Whether they're fighting a Dark wizard, getting back at a bully, or even helping with homework (okay, that's usually just Hermione), these friends always have one another's backs!

HERMIONE GRANGER

Hermione Granger is a Muggle-born witch who is considered the brightest in her class at Hogwarts. She can often be found with her nose in a book at the Hogwarts library, studying, doing homework, or even just reading for fun.

Hermione is so smart that she is given special permission to take extra classes in her third year at Hogwarts. Professor McGonagall gives Hermione a Time-Turner so she can take multiple classes at the same time. She may or may not also use that Time-Turner illegally to free one of the most wanted wizards in the world, Sirius Black—*cough, cough*—she totally does and it's awesome—*ahem*–but the point is, she learns a lot!

Hermione always has her hand up in class, and she is known for helping her best friends, Harry and Ron, with their homework. Some small-minded people think Hermione is less of a witch because she's Muggle-born. But it's clear from her many magical feats that nothing could be further from the truth!

FUN FACT: HERMIONE'S PARENTS ARE DENTISTS!

Hermione is a strict rule follower—most of the time. She knows that sometimes you have to break a rule or two to get something important done. And sometimes that rule breaking involves brewing an illegal Polyjuice Potion to help Harry and Ron transform into Slytherin students and get information about the monster in the Chamber of Secrets. Piece of cake! And even after that same monster turns Hermione to stone, she manages to get information to Harry and Ron that will help them defeat it. Honestly, without Hermione's brains, those boys would have been in big trouble in their first years at school!

Hermione also plays an important part in the search for Voldemort's Horcruxes—pieces of his soul that he concealed in precious objects. She helps Harry and Ron uncover clues and brings a lot of crucial supplies along on their journey—she has an enchanted purse that can fit books, clothing, and even a giant tent!

RON WEASLEY

Ron Weasley is the youngest boy in a family of seven children. He has five older brothers and one younger sister. Finding time to use the bathroom must be a competitive sport in the Weasley household!

Ron is often self-conscious because his family doesn't have a lot of money. He has to make do with hand-me-down robes, used books, and a pet rat named Scabbers that's been passed down from his brother Percy. Little does Ron know, Scabbers's age is the least of his worries: The rat is actually a wizard named Peter Pettigrew who's on the run from Voldemort! How's that for unwelcome hand-me-downs?

Despite their big family, the Weasleys are always willing to host a few more. Ron's best friends, Harry and Hermione, spend a lot of summers and holidays with Ron and his family. Harry and Hermione grew up with Muggles, so it's up to Ron to teach them everything they need to know about the Wizarding World. He introduces them to games like wizard chess (which is much livelier than Muggle chess) and wizard candy like Chocolate Frogs and Bertie Bott's Every Flavor Beans. And being the good friend he is, he warns Harry that Bertie Bott's *really* means every flavor—even booger flavored!

BIGGEST FEAR: SPIDERS

HOGWARTS HOUSE: GRYFFINDOR
IF IT LOOKS LIKE A RAT AND SMELLS LIKE A RAT—IT COULD STILL BE A FUGITIVE WIZARD IN DISGUISE!
FUN FACT: RON CAN'T BE BEAT DURING A GAME OF WIZARD CHESS!

RON WEASLEY
WE DIDN'T STEAL MY DAD'S CAR SO MUCH AS BORROW WITHOUT ASKING.

Whenever Harry Potter is in the middle of a dangerous adventure, Ron is usually right by his side. He plays a life-size game of wizard chess while protecting the Sorcerer's Stone and sacrifices his own piece so Harry can move on and defeat Voldemort. In their second year, Harry and Ron steal Mr. Weasley's flying car and use it to get to Hogwarts at the start of the term. It all goes exactly according to plan! Well, if part of their plan was to fly directly into the Whomping Willow and almost face injury by angry tree. And for Ron to get a Howler, a letter that projects his mother's furious voice for everyone in the Great Hall to hear what big trouble he's in. Be thankful Muggle parents don't have an invention like that!

In their sixth year, Harry and Ron are on the Gryffindor Quidditch team together. Harry is Captain, and he chooses Ron to be the Keeper. It takes some time for Ron to gain his confidence, but once he does, he's the star of the game! He helps the team win some exciting matches, including one against their biggest rival, the Slytherin team.

DRACO MALFOY

Every Chosen One needs a nemesis, right? Well, **Draco Malfoy** is Harry's. They are in the same year, and they get off to a bad start right away after Draco makes fun of Ron Weasley. Harry always blames Draco whenever something bad is happening, and the two boys often get each other in trouble.

Draco thinks he's better than other people because he comes from a pure-blood family with lots of money. Draco has two cronies—er, best friends—Crabbe and Goyle, who follow him around and agree with everything he says. Let's just say the two of them aren't the sharpest quills in the inkwell. But Draco is happy having people to boss around!

Draco's father, Lucius, is one of Voldemort's most loyal followers. Draco also becomes involved with Voldemort in his sixth year, but he doesn't like the things Voldemort makes him do. So it turns out he's not *pure* evil like Harry thought— maybe just about 72 percent evil. During the Battle of Hogwarts, Draco and his family decide to abandon Voldemort and go off on their own.

QUIDDITCH POSITION:
SEEKER

21

GINNY WEASLEY

Ginny Weasley is the youngest of the seven Weasley children and the only girl. Her six brothers love to tease her but are also very protective of her. She has had a crush on Harry ever since he became best friends with her brother Ron, so, naturally, she spends her first couple of years at school avoiding him and turning red when he speaks to her.

During Ginny's first year at Hogwarts, she is tricked into using Voldemort's old diary (from when he still went by the name Tom Riddle). Through the diary, Riddle makes Ginny do terrible things and leave threatening messages to the school. Then, at the end of the school year, she is taken into the Chamber of Secrets. Luckily, Harry is able to destroy the diary and save Ginny's life.

As Ginny grows up, she becomes less shy and proves herself to be a powerful witch. She's been known to produce a *Reducto* curse so powerful it turns solid objects to dust. Let's see some crusty old diary try to mess with her now! She is a member of Dumbledore's Army and fights alongside Harry and their friends at the Department of Mysteries in her fourth year.

FUN FACT: GINNY AND HARRY EVENTUALLY GET MARRIED!
I DON'T NEED MY BROTHERS TO HELP ME. I CAN PROTECT MYSELF!
PATRONUS: HORSE
QUIDDITCH POSITION: CHASER

NEVILLE LONGBOTTOM

Neville Longbottom is a Gryffindor in Harry's year at Hogwarts. In Neville's first year, his grandmother gets him a Remembrall, a device to help him figure out when he's forgotten something—which happens to Neville a lot. During a flying lesson, Draco Malfoy—yeah, *that* guy again—steals the Remembrall and flies away with it. Harry gets the ball back for Neville, and the two have been friends ever since.

Things always seem to go a little bit wrong for Neville. In his second year, when Professor Lockhart lets a cage of Cornish pixies loose in the classroom, the pixies grab Neville by the ears and tie him to a chandelier on the ceiling! Not his finest moment.

What Neville sometimes lacks in natural magical ability, he makes up for in loyalty and bravery. He joins Dumbledore's Army and he keeps the secret group running in his seventh year while Harry, Ron, and Hermione are away from Hogwarts. During the Battle of Hogwarts, Neville stands up to Voldemort himself, giving Harry an opening to defeat He-Who-Must-Not-Be-Named once and for all.

EPIC MOMENT: WHEN NEVILLE
FEATS VOLDEMORT'S SNAKE WITH
THE SWORD OF GRYFFINDOR!

FAVORITE SUBJECT: HERBOLOGY

PET: A TOAD NAMED TREVOR

OLIVER WOOD

Oliver Wood is the Captain of the Gryffindor Quidditch team during Harry's first three years at Hogwarts. He plays the position of Keeper, so he is responsible for blocking the other team from scoring a goal. You don't want to face Oliver in front of a Quidditch hoop! When Professor McGonagall catches Harry doing some risky flying his first time on a broomstick, unsupervised, she gives him a detention—just kidding; Professor McGonagall, Head of Gryffindor House, loves to win! She recommends Harry for the Quidditch team and introduces him to Oliver.

Quidditch is a little different than most Muggle sports, considering it's played on broomsticks, and Oliver teaches Harry all about it. He explains the different players: the Keeper, the Chasers, the Beaters, and the Seeker. Then he shows Harry all the different balls used during a match: a Quaffle, two Bludgers, and the Golden Snitch.

Calling Oliver competitive would be an understatement. His number one goal is for the Gryffindor team to win the Quidditch Cup. Before each match, he gives a really, really, really, really long pep talk. Even though he can get a bit, well, *overenthusiastic*, Oliver helps Harry become an excellent Quidditch player and teaches him how to be a great team captain.

HOGWARTS HOUSE:
GRYFFINDOR
THE MOST IMPORTANT THING ABOUT PLAYING QUIDDITCH IS WINNING—ER, I MEAN, HAVING FUN.
EPIC MOMENT:
WHEN HE MAKES
ANY AMAZING SAVES,
ESPECIALLY DURING
ANY MATCH AGAINST
SLYTHERIN!
QUIDDITCH POSITION:
KEEPER

CEDRIC DIGGORY

Cedric Diggory is a popular student a few years older than Harry. When Hogwarts hosts the Triwizard Tournament, Cedric is chosen from the Goblet of Fire as the champion to compete for Hogwarts. Then Harry's name comes out of the goblet, too, making him the surprise fourth champion. Even ancient enchanted goblets make mistakes!

Most of the school supports Cedric as their only champion because they think Harry is in the tournament unfairly. And come on, Harry gets enough attention already! But Cedric and Harry help each other with the tournament. Before the second task, Cedric hints that Harry should take a bath—not because he's smelly, but because it would help him discover a crucial clue. And, okay, those flower-scented bubbles are also pretty relaxing.

When the two boys are tied in the final task, they decide to share the Triwizard Cup. The cup transports them to a spooky cemetery where Voldemort is waiting—it was all a trap to catch Harry! Leave it to Voldemort to punish students for showing some nice sportsmanship.

I DO
ALL MY BEST
NKING IN A BUBBLE
TH. ALSO, THAT'S HOW
MY HAIR STAYS SO
SHINY.
FUN FACT: CEDRIC ATTENDS THE YULE BALL WITH CHO CHANG.
QUIDDITCH POSITION: SEEKER
OGWARTS HOUSE: FFLEPUFF
I
WIZ
ARD

FUNNIEST MOMENT:

WHEN HARRY TRIES TO SMILE AT CHO FROM ACROSS THE GREAT HALL—BUT ENDS UP SPILLING WATER ALL OVER HIMSELF!

Cho Chang is a Ravenclaw student and Harry's first crush! Their eyes meet one day over the Pumpkin Pasties on the Hogwarts Express, and it is love at first sight . . . well, actually, not so much. When Harry asks Cho to attend the Yule Ball with him in his fourth year, Cho says no because she's already going with Cedric Diggory. That's right, even Mr. "Chosen One" himself gets turned down for a date!

The next year, Harry and Cho finally get together, but it doesn't last very long. After Professor Umbridge tricks Cho into drinking tea that contains a truth-telling potion, Cho reveals the secret meeting location for Dumbledore's Army. Harry is too upset to hear her side of the story and they stop speaking. Eventually, the two become friends again and Cho fights alongside Harry and their classmates in the Battle of Hogwarts.

HOGWARTS HOUSE: RAVENCLAW

FRED AND GEORGE WEASLEY

Fred and George are identical twins and the middle Weasley children. They're the family jokesters, often cooking up mischievous pranks to play on their siblings or fellow Hogwarts students. Everyone knows to be careful if the Weasley twins offer up any sweets—those treats could be disguised as something else!

Fred and George drop out of Hogwarts during their seventh year to open their own joke shop in Diagon Alley, **Weasleys' Wizard Wheezes**. But before they leave school, they make sure they go out with a bang—literally! They set off hundreds of fireworks inside the school, including some that chase the loathed Professor Umbridge through the halls.

At Weasleys' Wizard Wheezes, they sell all kinds of products of their own invention including Extendable Ears (for eavesdropping), Skiving Snackboxes (for getting out of a boring class), and Decoy Detonators (for causing a distraction). Harry Potter gives the twins the money to start their store, so they let him have any product he wants for free—a perk they do NOT offer to their own brother, Ron, much to his outrage.

QUIDDITCH POSITIONS: BEATERS

EPIC MOMENT:

WHEN THEY SET OFF FIREWORKS IN THE MIDDLE OF EXAMS.

FUN FACT:

FRED AND GEORGE'S JOKE INVENTIONS HAVE OFTEN HELPED HARRY POTTER CARRY OUT HIGHLY IMPORTANT MISSIONS.

LUNA LOVEGOOD

Luna Lovegood meets Harry, Ron, Hermione, and Neville when they all ride the carriage to the castle together at the start of the school year. Luna bonds with Harry because they are the only two people who can see the mysterious creatures that are pulling the carriage. This realization is not a comfort to Harry, considering the fact that other students refer to Luna as "Loony" Lovegood. Not really someone you want to be sharing strange visions with!

But Luna doesn't mind—she just wants to be herself. She wears jewelry to keep away Nargles, creatures that most wizards consider made-up. She also wears funny-shaped glasses called Spectrespecs to help her see Wrackspurts, which is *another* creature most wizards don't believe in. (Dragons and mermaids are all fine, though.)

Luna soon becomes close friends with Harry and the others. She is also an important member of Dumbledore's Army, and she goes with Harry to fight Voldemort's followers at the Department of Mysteries.

FAVORITE MAGAZINE: *THE QUIBBLER*

OF COURSE I'VE NEVER SEEN A NARGLE. MY NECKLACE KEEPS THEM AWAY, AFTER ALL!

THE QUIBBLER
PANDEMONIUM at THE MINISTRY
UNFUZZ THE MYSTERY

HOGWARTS HOUSE: RAVENCLAW

PATRONUS: HARE

Seamus Finnigan is a Gryffindor student in Harry's year. He starts off his Hogwarts education with a bang—literally! Somehow, Seamus's spells often have a way of ending with something exploding. In Charms class, the feather he is trying to make levitate blows up instead. Hopefully he didn't do the same thing on his end-of-year exam!

Seamus and Harry sleep in the same dorm and are good friends—Seamus even paints "Potter" on his forehead to support Harry in the Triwizard Tournament! But when the news of Voldemort's return to power is first revealed, there are many in the Wizarding World who doubt Harry's story—including Seamus. They have a big fight and don't speak for a long time. Eventually, Seamus comes around and apologizes to Harry, even joining Dumbledore's Army with his best friend, Dean. Good thing, too—wouldn't want someone whose spells are so unpredictable fighting for the other side!

HOGWARTS HOUSE:
GRYFFINDOR

DEAN THOMAS

SEAMUS AN[D]
DO EVERYTH[ING]
TOGETHER—
INCLUDING PROTEC[T]
HOGWARTS FRO[M]
BAD GUYS!

Dean Thomas is another Gryffindor in Harry's year and Seamus Finnigan's best friend. Whether they're hanging out in the Gryffindor common room or eating together in the Great Hall, Seamus and Dean are always together. But that doesn't mean they agree on everything. When Seamus is convinced Harry isn't telling the truth about Voldemort's return, Dean still chooses to join Dumbledore's Army with Harry, Ron, and Hermione.

In Dean's sixth year at Hogwarts, he begins dating Ginny Weasley—a fact that her brother Ron is not particularly happy about! Dean and Ron are friends, but Ron is very protective of his sister. To Ron's relief, eventually they break up (little does Ron know, Ginny will date his very BEST friend next).

Dean joins his classmates in the Battle of Hogwarts. In the aftermath of an exhausting battle, he's found—where else?—drinking tea and laughing with his good old buddy Seamus.

HOGWARTS HOUSE:
GRYFFINDOR

HOGWARTS STAFF

Hogwarts School of Witchcraft and Wizardry is staffed by many brilliant and experienced witches and wizards. The professors are responsible for teaching magic to the next generation, and they take his job very seriously. They don't want a bunch of kids who can't even cast a Summoning Charm running loose with wands!

Students from all four of the Hogwarts houses take a number of classes each year, including Potions, Transfiguration, Charms, Defense Against the Dark Arts, History of Magic, and Herbology. As they get older, students can choose to take additional classes as well, like Care of Magical Creatures, Divination, Arithmancy, and even Muggle Studies. That's right: somewhere, a wizard might be bent over his textbook studying why YOU take a bath with your rubber ducky.

Four professors serve as the heads of houses for Gryffindor, Slytherin, Ravenclaw, and Hufflepuff. While some teachers have been at Hogwarts for many years, others—like the Defense Against the Dark Arts professors—seem to last only one year before leaving. Whether they are giving out detentions, helping a student, or defending the castle from enemies, these professors are the top of their class.

ALBUS DUMBLEDORE

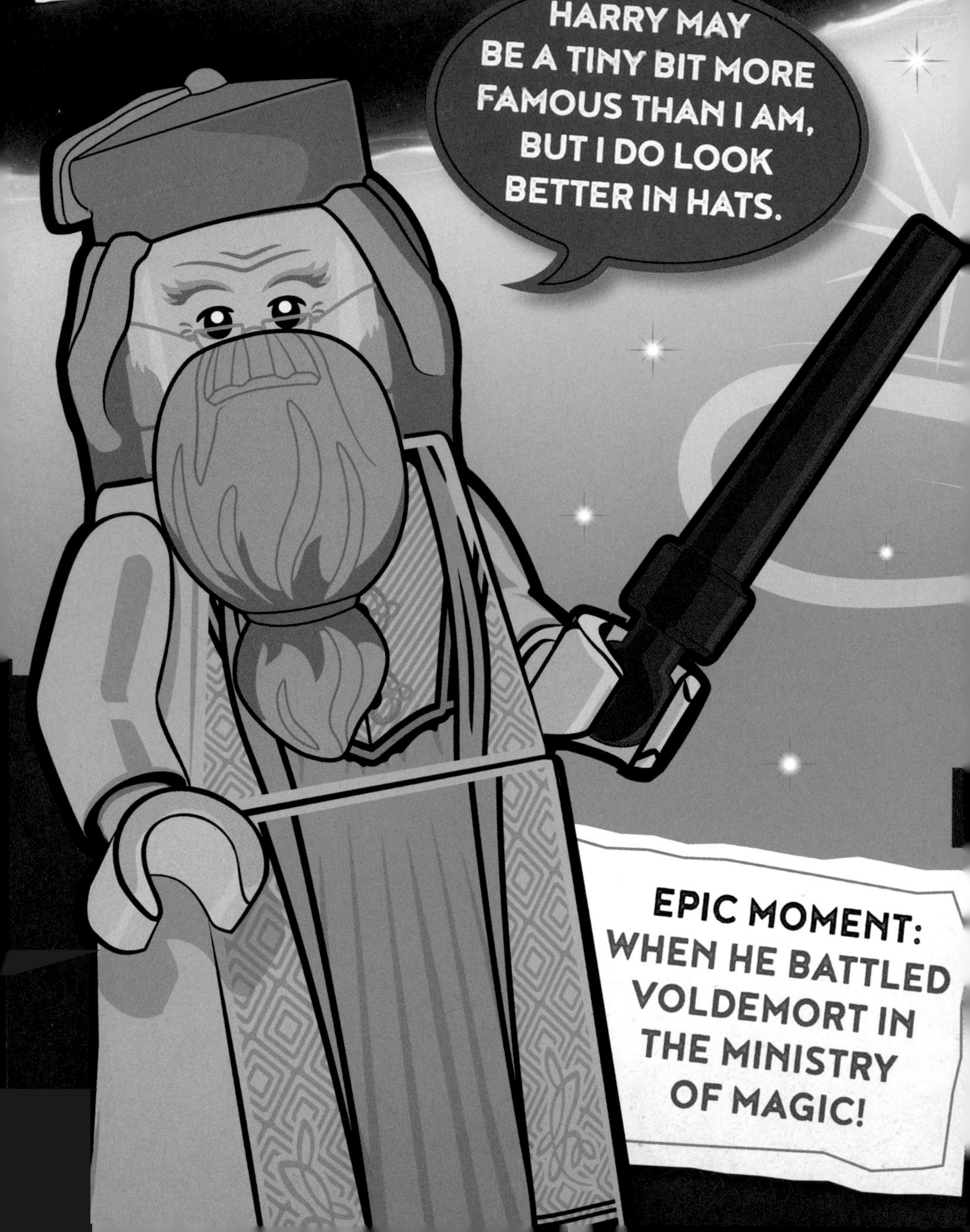

Albus Dumbledore is the headmaster at Hogwarts and the founder of the Order of the Phoenix, a secret group dedicated to fighting Voldemort. He is one of the most powerful (and famous!) people in the Wizarding World. He's even featured on a Chocolate Frog card, so you know he's a big deal!

Some of Dumbledore's greatest achievements include his discovery of different uses of dragon's blood, alchemical work with Nicholas Flamel (the creator of the Sorcerer's Stone), and his defeat of the powerful Dark wizard Gellert Grindelwald. Not to mention, he has a pretty impressive beard!

As headmaster of Hogwarts, Dumbledore gives speeches at every school feast and awards points for the House Cup. He also deals with serious disciplinary matters when a student does something against the rules—though some at Hogwarts think he goes a bit easier on Harry Potter and his friends than other students who get into trouble.

FULL NAME: ALBUS PERCIVAL WULFRIC BRIAN DUMBLEDORE

ALBUS
DUMBLEDORE

Professor Dumbledore and Harry are very close. It's Dumbledore who leaves baby Harry on the Dursleys' doorstep after his parents are attacked by Voldemort. Nice going, Albus—those guys are the worst! But Dumbledore is all wise and mysterious and has his reasons for making Harry live with them.

In Harry's first year, Dumbledore anonymously gives Harry an invisibility cloak for Christmas. He may as well have said, "Here you go, Harry, the perfect item to help you disguise yourself and break every school rule we have! Enjoy!" Dumbledore also teaches Harry about the power of the Mirror of Erised. Harry spends several nights sitting in front of the magical mirror so he can see his family, but Dumbledore warns Harry not to dwell on the past. (Though Dumbledore probably still dreams about those delicious Pumpkin Pasties he had at Christmas ten years ago.)

TEACHERS SHOULDN'T HAVE FAVORITE STUDENTS . . . BUT I'M THE HEADMASTER SO I CHOOSE HARRY.

Dumbledore begins private lessons with Harry in his sixth year. Dumbledore uses these lessons to teach Harry about Voldemort's past and how Harry can defeat him.

MINERVA MCGONAGALL

Minerva McGonagall is the Transfiguration professor. She teaches the students how to change objects from one thing to another (like a bird into a teacup—you never know when you might have an impromptu tea party). She is also the Head of Gryffindor house.

Professor McGonagall is one of the strictest professors at Hogwarts, but she's also one of the most loyal. You definitely want her on your side in a fight, like when she stands up to Professor Umbridge for her severe Ministry Decrees. If Professor McGonagall thinks you're being too strict, you know it's pretty bad!

Professor McGonagall is also an accomplished Animagus. She can transform into a cat that has markings just like her real glasses! After Harry survives Lord Voldemort's attack as a baby, Professor McGonagall stays in cat form all day to spy on Harry's Muggle family—a good disguise, since cats always look like they're up to something suspicious anyway.

TRANSFIGURATION IS THE PURR-FECT SUBJECT.

EPIC MOMENT:

WHEN SHE BRINGS THE STATUES AND SUITS OF ARMOR TO LIFE DURING THE BATTLE OF HOGWARTS!

PATRONUS: CAT

47

SEVERUS SNAPE

PATRONUS: DOE

Severus Snape is the Potions master at Hogwarts. He is also the Head of Slytherin house. In Harry's sixth year, Snape finally gets the job he's always wanted: Defense Against the Dark Arts professor. But like everyone else before him, he teaches that subject for only one year.

Professor Snape is feared by many students, and it's no wonder—would it hurt to wear a pop of color or even smile once in a while? He shows favoritism to his Slytherin students, like Draco Malfoy, but is unfair and even cruel to many other students. When Neville Longbottom sees a Boggart in his third year, it reveals his greatest fear is Professor Snape! Other students' greatest fears include spiders, giant snakes, and Dementors—not the best company to find yourself in.

From their first Potions lesson together, Snape and Harry don't get along. Harry always thinks that Snape is up to something, even when Dumbledore assures Harry that Snape is one of the good guys. In Harry's first year, he, Ron, and Hermione are convinced that Snape is trying to steal the Sorcerer's Stone. It turns out that Snape is actually protecting the Stone. Easy mistake, guys, it could have happened to anyone!

FUN FACT: SNAPE IS SKILLED AT OCCLUMENCY: A KIND OF MAGICAL MIND-READING.

49

SEVERUS SNAPE

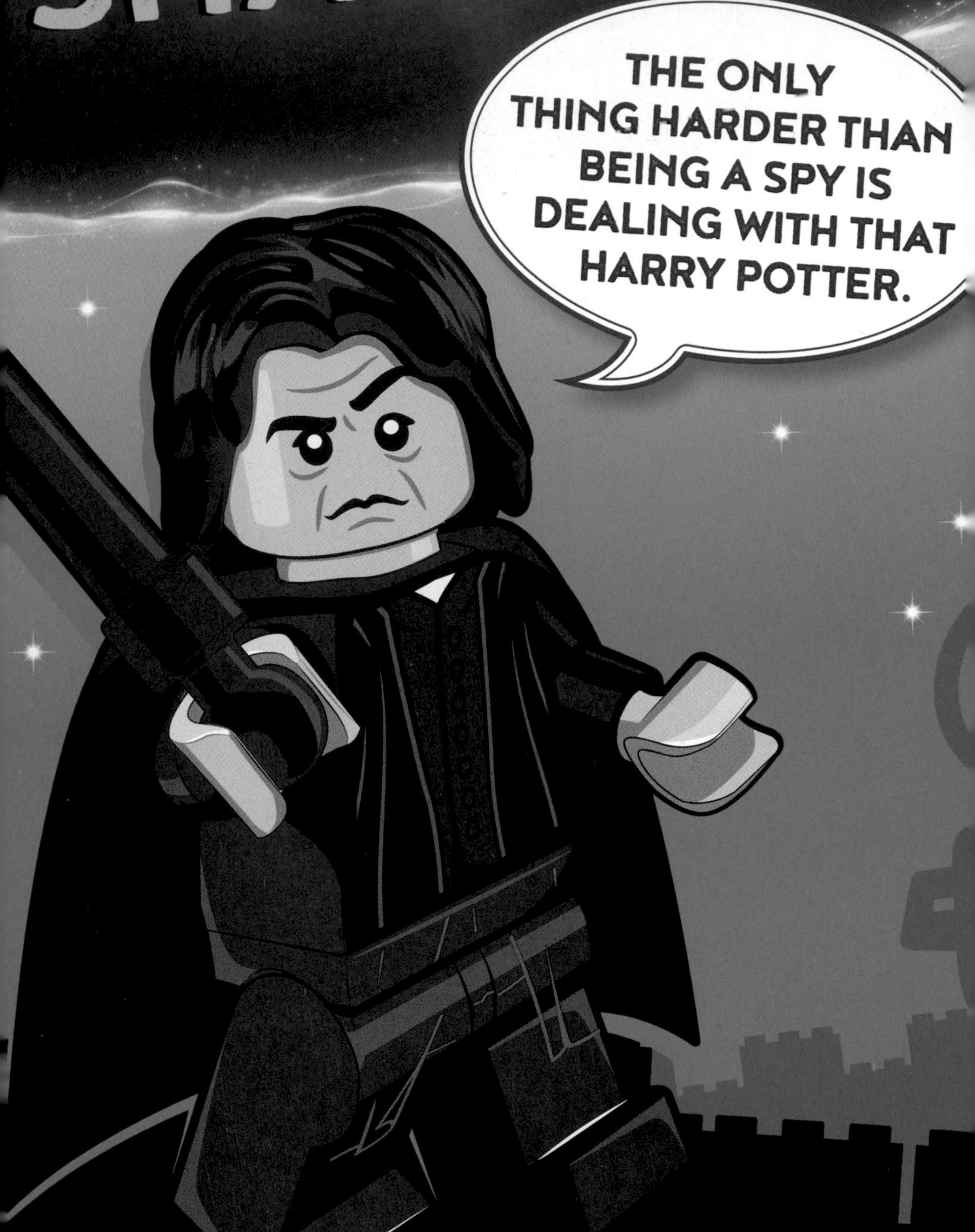

Professor Snape is also an important member of the Order of the Phoenix. Snape used to follow Voldemort's orders but he realized that he was on the wrong side. He volunteers to be a spy for the Order instead.

Once Voldemort returns to power, Snape pretends to be loyal to him again. He tells Voldemort that he will report on what Dumbledore and the Order are up to. Really, Snape is secretly working for the good guys—but that still doesn't stop him from being super grumpy to everyone!

It's hard for some people to tell which side Snape is on, including Harry. In the end, it becomes clear that even though Snape definitely won't be winning any "Most Friendly" awards around Hogwarts any time soon, he does want Voldemort to be defeated.

RUBEUS HAGRID

Rubeus Hagrid is the Keeper of the Keys and Grounds at Hogwarts. He is the first person from the Wizarding World Harry Potter meets, and he makes quite the impression. Hagrid comes to Harry on his eleventh birthday and tells him that he is a wizard—talk about a birthday surprise! He takes Harry shopping in Diagon Alley and even buys him a pet owl.

Hagrid is a member of the Order of the Phoenix and he works closely with Dumbledore. When Hagrid was a student at Hogwarts, he was framed for unleashing the monster in the Chamber of Secrets and then expelled. Because of his past, others question why Dumbledore trusts Hagrid so much. And let's face it, Hagrid isn't doing himself any favors by making his love for all creatures, no matter how dangerous, known. He did hatch a (fire-breathing) dragon egg in his own (wooden) cabin!

But Dumbledore knows that Hagrid has a good heart, and he hires him as the Care of Magical Creatures professor in Harry's third year. Hagrid is thrilled and can't wait to teach his students about all the creatures he finds most fascinating. The problem is, what he calls fascinating, most others call *terrifying*!

HOGWARTS HOUSE: GRYFFINDOR

PET: A GIANT DOG NAMED FANG

53

QUIRINUS QUIRRELL

Quirinus Quirrell is the Defense Against the Dark Arts teacher at Hogwarts during Harry's first year. He is very nervous, stutters, and wears a purple turban. What the students don't know is that the turban hides Lord Voldemort in the back of his head! Now that's a scary hairstyle. Voldemort wants Quirrell to steal the Sorcerer's Stone for him so that he can regain his true form and power.

First, Quirrell tries to steal the Stone from Gringotts bank, which was his first mistake. Gringotts is one of the most secure places in the entire Wizarding World! Then, when the Stone is taken to Hogwarts, he tries to steal it from the school. But Hogwarts is the other most secure place in the entire Wizarding World! Apparently, this guy hasn't read *Hogwarts: A History.* Quirrell lets a troll into the castle on Halloween to cause a diversion, but Snape stops him from getting the stone. Nice try, buddy.

Quirrell has to drink unicorn's blood in the Forbidden Forest to keep Voldemort alive—but he's still no match for Harry Potter. Harry stops him from stealing the Stone and Quirrell is never to be seen again.

FAVORITE SUBJECT:

DEFENSE AGAINST THE DARK ARTS

FUNNIEST MOMENT:

WHEN QUIRRELL FAINTS IN THE GREAT HALL AFTER TELLING EVERYONE ABOUT THE TROLL!

FUN FACT:
QUIRRELL IS HARRY'S FIRST DEFENSE AGAINST THE DARK ARTS TEACHER—HE HAS A NEW ONE EVERY YEAR!

REMUS LUPIN
THERE'S NOTHING THAT CHOCOLATE CAN'T F
WELL, EXCEPT FOR
WEREWOLF BITE.
ALSO KNOWN AS: "MOONY"

FAVORITE REMEDY: CHOCOLATE

Remus Lupin is the Defense Against the Dark Arts professor at Hogwarts during Harry's third year. He teaches the students about interesting—and often spooky—creatures like Boggarts, Grindylows, Dementors, and more.

Lupin meets Harry on the Hogwarts Express when Dementors board the train and suck all happiness and good feelings away. He gives Harry lots of chocolate to make him feel better—maybe Muggle doctors should try the same thing! They begin having private lessons so that Harry can learn how to cast a Patronus Charm to keep Dementors away.

Lupin was best friends with Harry's father, James; Sirius Black; and Peter Pettigrew during their days at Hogwarts. Professor Lupin was bitten by a werewolf when he was a child, so his friends learned how to transform into animals so they could still be with him during the full moon. Friends that howl at the moon together stay together!

Professor Snape makes Lupin a potion to control his werewolf behavior and keep his condition a secret while he works at Hogwarts. But when he misses a dose, he transforms on the castle grounds. After Lupin's secret gets out, he resigns from his teaching job. Adiós to another Defense Against the Dark Arts teacher!

HOGWARTS HOUSE: GRYFFINDOR

SYBIL TRELAWNEY

Sybil Trelawney is the Divination professor at Hogwarts. In Divination, students learn how to predict the future (or try to, anyway). They gaze into crystal balls, consult the stars, and read tea leaves. But many of Trelawney's students do not have "the gift of sight." Harry and Ron spend a lot of time making things up, and Hermione drops the class after deciding it's all nonsense.

EPIC MOMENT: WHEN TRELAWNEY PREDICTS VOLDEMORT'S RETURN!

CRYSTAL GAZING IS A USEFUL ART . . . I ALWAYS KNOW WHEN TO BRING AN UMBRELLA!

TRADEMARK LOOK: GIANT ROUND GLASSES AND LOTS OF SCARVES—STYLISH AND COZY!

Most of Professor Trelawney's predictions don't really come true—but she *has* made two accurate prophecies! First, before Harry was born, she predicted that a baby born at the end of July would be the one to defeat Voldemort. Then in Harry's third year, she predicts that Lord Voldemort's servant will return to him—and that night, Peter Pettigrew does! If only she had predicted that Voldemort had a change of heart and decided to focus on his vegetable garden instead . . .

FUN FACT: DIVINATION CLASSES ARE HELD IN ONE OF THE HIGH TOWERS OF HOGWARTS CASTLE.

FILIUS FLITWICK

Filius Flitwick is the Charms professor at Hogwarts. He is also the Head of Ravenclaw house. Professor Flitwick is very short, so he often stands on top of a tall pile of books when teaching his classes. (Don't tell the Hogwarts librarian!)

In Charms class, Professor Flitwick teaches his students spells to make things levitate, fly, and move—like the Summoning Charm, which makes an object zoom toward you. That would sure come in handy when the remote control is just out of reach!

When he's not teaching Charms classes or spending time in Ravenclaw Tower, Professor Flitwick is also the conductor for the Hogwarts choir. During the Battle of Hogwarts, Flitwick plays an important role in the castle's defense. He helps cast a giant shield charm around the castle to keep out Voldemort's army.

HOGWARTS HOUSE:
RAVENCLAW

SWISH AND FLICK, THAT'S WHAT I ALWAYS SAY!
FUN FACT: FLITWICK'S CHOIR ONCE SANG WITH GIANT TOADS!
SPECIAL SKILL: DECORATING THE HOGWARTS CHRISTMAS TREE USING A LEVITATION CHARM

POMONA SPROUT

Pomona Sprout is the Herbology professor and Head of Hufflepuff house at Hogwarts. Her classes are held in greenhouses out on the castle grounds. In Herbology, students learn how to care for and use a variety of magical plants and fungi. It may sound dull, but this isn't like your neighbor's gardening: some of those plants have minds of their own!

In one memorable Herbology lesson, the class learns how to repot Mandrakes. Mandrakes are plants that look like ugly babies—no wonder they cry so much!

Professor Sprout uses some of her most dangerous plants to help the school. In Harry's first year, she sets up a trap of Devil's Snare to protect the precious Sorcerer's Stone. And when the Basilisk from the Chamber of Secrets turns students to stone, Professor Sprout uses her Mandrake plants to revive them. Thank Merlin for those ugly baby plants!

HOGWARTS HOUSE:
HUFFLEPUFF

FAVORITE SUBJECT:
HERBOLOG
(NATURALLY

WHO HAS TWO GREEN THUMBS AND LOVES PLANTS? THIS WITCH!

FUN FACT: MANY OF PROFESSOR SPROUT'S PLANTS ARE USED AS REMEDIES IN THE HOSPITAL WING.

GILDEROY LOCKHART

Gilderoy Lockhart is the most famous person in the Wizarding World—well, according to him, that is. He's the author of many books about his own travels and accomplishments, as well as his autobiography, *Magical Me*.

In Harry's second year, Lockhart is hired to teach Defense Against the Dark Arts at Hogwarts. But the skills he writes about in his books don't exactly translate into successfully teaching students . . . During his first class, Lockhart releases a cage full of mischievous pixies and then leaves Harry and his friends to deal with them alone. And they don't even get extra credit!

Lockhart is always boasting about how he has defeated creatures like ghouls, trolls, and vampires. But Harry and Ron discover that Lockhart is slimier than Ron's backfiring slug spell! He actually steals his impressive stories from other witches and wizards and then wipes their memories so he can take all the credit. Long story short, when one of Lockhart's own Memory Charms backfires on himself, no one feels all that bad for him.

FUN FACT:
LOCKHART IS A FIVE-TIME WINNER OF *WITCH WEEKLY*'S MOST CHARMING SMILE AWARD.

FUNNIEST MOMENT:
WHEN A SWARM OF PIXIES TRY TO STEAL LOCKHART'S PAINTING OF HIMSELF!

FAVORITE CHARM:
THE MEMORY-WIPING CHARM, ***OBLIVIATE***

Horace Slughorn is the Potions master at Hogwarts during Harry's sixth year. He was Head of Slytherin house when he first taught at Hogwarts, back when Voldemort was still a student known as Tom Riddle. Slughorn came out of retirement to return to Hogwarts at Dumbledore's request—it's really hard to say no to that guy!

Professor Slughorn invites promising students to his Slug Club, which is much cooler than it sounds. The Slug Club is for students with impressive skills or well-connected family members. Slughorn hosts dinners and parties for the Slug Club so he can keep in touch with the students over the years. Harry, Hermione, Neville, and Ginny are invited to Slughorn's first dinner after returning to Hogwarts. Maybe Ron's invitation was, uh, lost in the Owl Post . . .

Harry spends a lot of time with Professor Slughorn to find out a secret he's hiding that could help defeat Voldemort. Harry eventually discovers that Professor Slughorn is the one who taught Voldemort about Horcruxes when he was still a student—talk about a big mistake!

FAVORITE SUBJECT: POTIONS

DOLORES UMBRIDGE

Dolores Umbridge is the Defense Against the Dark Arts professor during Harry's fifth year at Hogwarts. There's just one *tiny* problem: she doesn't allow any of her students to perform defensive spells!

The Ministry of Magic sends Umbridge to Hogwarts to keep Dumbledore from spreading the story of Voldemort's return. She is named High Inquisitor, which gives her the power to enforce strict rules, like banning student organizations and all joke products from Fred and George Weasley.

Umbridge leaves Hogwarts after the Ministry finally accepts that Voldemort has returned. But Harry and his friends can't get rid of her that easily. A couple years later, they must retrieve one of Voldemort's Horcruxes that also happens to be Umbridge's new necklace. They go undercover and snatch the Horcrux right off her neck. Evil is never in style!

MADAME HOOCH

Madame Hooch teaches Flying lessons to all first year students at Hogwarts. In Harry's first lesson, he proves to be a natural on a broomstick. Poor Neville Longbottom is another story . . .

Neville loses control of his broom and it carries him all around the castle, eventually dropping him on the ground. Madame Hooch has to rush him to the hospital wing, warning the other students not to get on their brooms while she's gone. But what she doesn't know is asking Harry to resist flying is like asking Snape to use some shampoo once in a while!

Madame Hooch is also the referee for all Quidditch matches, meaning she has the difficult job of breaking up arguments between certain teams who may not get along (*ahem*, usually Slytherin and Gryffindor). She always insists that the team Captains shake hands and then releases the Quidditch balls into the air, starting the match.

FAVORITE SPORT:
QUIDDITCH

EPIC MOMENT:
WHEN SHE ANNOUNCES GRYFFINDOR'S BIG WIN AGAINST SLYTHERIN IN HARRY'S FIRST MATCH!

ARGUS FILCH

IN MY DAY, THERE WAS NO LAUGHTER ALLOWED IN THE HALLS!

FUNNIEST MOMENT: WHEN FILCH BALLROOM DANCES WITH MRS. NORRIS AT THE YULE BALL!

Argus Filch is Hogwarts's caretaker. He's responsible for making sure the castle stays in tip-top shape—so he's really not happy when students track mud from outside into the Great Hall! Filch never misses a chance to scold the students or try and put them in detention. His beloved cat, Mrs. Norris, often prowls around the castle at night, ready to alert Filch if she sees a student out of bed after hours. The students fear Mrs. Norris almost as much as her grouchy owner!

FUN FACT: THE WEASLEY TWINS STOLE THE MARAUDER'S MAP FROM FILCH'S OFFICE IN THEIR FIRST YEAR.

Filch becomes head of Professor Umbridge's Inquisitorial Squad in Harry's fifth year. He, along with a group of Slytherin students, enforce Umbridge's impossibly strict rules. Filch is also determined to catch a meeting of the secret group Dumbledore's Army in action, but the students know how to outsmart him. All it takes is a strategically placed box of seemingly innocent chocolates to make Filch break out in boils and distract him from his mission!

HOGWARTS FOUNDERS

Hogwarts was founded a long time ago by a small group of gifted witches and wizards: Rowena Ravenclaw, Helga Hufflepuff, Godric Gryffindor, and Salazar Slytherin. These four friends wanted to crea a safe place for young witches and wizards to learn magic, away from the prying eyes of nosy Muggles.

The founders each created their own houses, named after themselves. Wouldn't you do the same? They each had different opinions about what characteristics make a great student, and they believed separating the students into houses would allow everyone to learn side by side in harmony. But Slytherin continued to disagree with the other three founders about who would be admitted to Hogwarts and eventually Slytherin left the school.

Hundreds of years after the founders began Hogwarts, their legacy still lives on in the school's many traditions, like the House Cup and the Sorting Ceremony. The values of each founder are carried on through the students in each house—including the house rivalries.

ROWENA RAVENCLAW

HELGA HUFFLEPUFF

GODRIC GRYFFINDOR

SALAZAR SLYTHERIN

Helga Hufflepuff was the Hogwarts founder you'd most likely want to sit and have a cup of tea with. When they created Hogwarts, the other three founders were very strict about the students they would allow in their houses. Hufflepuff thought every magical child should have an equal chance to learn, so she was happy to welcome anyone into her house—though she especially valued those who were hardworking, loyal, and always played fair.

Hufflepuff had a treasured golden cup that she passed down through her family. Voldemort eventually stole the cup and made it into a Horcrux, an evil magical invention that would help him live longer. Years later, Hermione Granger destroys the cup Horcrux with a Basilisk fang during the epic Battle of Hogwarts!

HOUSE SYMBOL: BADGER

ROWENA RAVENCLAW

Rowena Ravenclaw wanted all students in her house to be intelligent, wise, and creative—in other words, nothing less than the very top of the class. No pressure or anything!

Rowena had a daughter named Helena, who eventually became the ghost of Ravenclaw Tower at Hogwarts. Students call her the Gray Lady. During the Battle of Hogwarts, Harry Potter discovers the Gray Lady's real name, revealing a deep secret she has kept for years. While Helena was still alive, she stole her mother's beloved diadem, a super-fancy word for a super-fancy crown with lots of jewels. The mystery of the diadem's location became part of wizarding folklore. One year at Hogwarts, a charming young student persuaded the Gray Lady to tell him where it was hidden . . . that student was Tom Riddle, aka young Voldemort! Bet you saw that one coming. Voldemort turned the diadem into a Horcrux and hid it deep inside Hogwarts. It was finally destroyed in a terrible fire in the Room of Requirement.

PRIZED POSSESSION:
DIADEM

HOUSE COLORS:
SILVER & BLUE

MY DAUGHTER WON'T STOP BORROWING THINGS FROM MY CLOSET!

HOUSE SYMBOL:
RAVEN

Salazar Slytherin is notorious for being the one Hogwarts founder who did not get along with the others. They all started as great friends, but the friendship took a horrible turn after Slytherin's true colors were revealed. Slytherin wanted his house full of students who were ambitious, cunning, and resourceful. Then, he wanted to accept only students with pureblood heritage.

The other founders did not agree, and they all had a big argument that ended in Slytherin leaving the school completely—but not before leaving his own mark that would last well after he was gone. He created the Chamber of Secrets, a secret dungeon deep below the school where a giant snake called a Basilisk lived. Most people would just leave a note or something, but Slytherin was clearly feeling a bit dramatic at the time. In Harry Potter's second year at Hogwarts, the Chamber is opened and the Basilisk attacks Muggle-born students. Harry defeats the Basilisk and makes Hogwarts safe for Muggle-borns once again. Salazar Slytherin had a heavy silver locket that eventually became one of Voldemort's Horcruxes. Ron Weasley destroys the Horcrux—and the locket—with the sword that once belonged to Slytherin's former friend: Godric Gryffindor.

HOUSE SYMBOL: SERPENT

GODRIC
GRYFFINDOR

Godric Gryffindor's house is for students who are courageous and daring, and maybe also the tiniest bit show-off-y. Gryffindors are leaders who love to take charge and often run headfirst into dangerous situations. It's certainly no surprise that Harry Potter is a Gryffindor!

Gryffindor had a valuable goblin-made sword that helps destroy many of Voldemort's Horcruxes. Harry Potter also uses the sword to defeat the Basilisk in the Chamber of Secrets after it magically appears inside the Sorting Hat. Harry later learns that the sword would only present itself to a true Gryffindor. Gryffindor's birthplace is named Godric's Hollow. Centuries after Gryffindor's birth, another very famous wizard is born in Godric's Hollow. That's right: it was Harry Potter.

PRIZED POSSESSION:
THE SWORD OF GRYFFINDOR

Some witches and wizards use their magic to steal, trick, and hurt others. Those who are caught spend time in Azkaban Prison, which is guarded by the soul-sucking Dementors. They drain all happiness from the people around them. Makes being grounded to your room seem not so bad anymore, right?!

While there have been many Dark wizards, the most infamous of all is Lord Voldemort. Most in the Wizarding World are so afraid of him that they refuse to even speak his name. He and his supporters spread misery to the Wizarding World for many years.

Voldemort's followers are marked by a tattoo of the Dark Mark. Voldemort can use this mark to communicate with his followers. Apparently sending out a group text doesn't have the same spooky effect. Despite Voldemort's power, good magic always overcomes the bad guys in the end!

Lord Voldemort was born with the name Tom Riddle. He is a descendent of Salazar Slytherin, one of the founders of Hogwarts, and he inherited Slytherin's ability to talk to snakes. Tom could have saved this cool power to use as a fun party trick, but, unfortunately, as we all know, he decided to take it in a different direction.

ALSO KNOWN AS:
"THE DARK LORD,"
"HE WHO MUST NOT BE NAMED,"
"YOU-KNOW-WHO," AND "TOM RIDDLE"

Tom attends Hogwarts, and on the outside, he is a model student. Most people are fooled by his act. He opens the Chamber of Secrets at Hogwarts and unleashes the giant serpent within on his fellow students, but Hagrid is the one expelled for the crime. This incident is just the beginning of Tom's Dark magic.

PET:
GIANT SNAKE NAMED NAGINI

After his rise to power, Tom begins to go by his new name: Lord Voldemort. (Most agree: Not really an improvement there.) When he learns of a prophecy that says Harry Potter is the only one who can defeat him, he attacks the Potter house. But Voldemort's curse on baby Harry rebounds. Voldemort is temporarily defeated, and Harry becomes the first and only person to survive the Avada Kedavra Curse, making him instantly famous. Definitely not what Voldemort was hoping would happen!

LORD VOLDEMORT

Throughout the years, rather than accepting a nice retirement on a tropical island where he can work on his much-needed tan, Lord Voldemort tries many different ways to regain his power and human form. He finally succeeds in Harry's fourth year with help from Peter Pettigrew. (Remember him? Also known as Scabbers!) Harry witnesses Voldemort's return, but at first, no one believes him. So Voldemort is able to recruit his old followers to return to his side.

Voldemort is so hard to defeat because he creates seven Horcruxes. Each of these Horcruxes contains a piece of Voldemort's soul, and they allow him to live even if his human body is destroyed. Basically, Voldemort is like a video game character with seven lives! Pretty cool—or, it would be if it weren't for the fact that he's using those lives to try and take over the Wizarding World and destroy whoever gets in his way. Voldemort hides his Horcruxes in important magical objects, like items that belonged to the four founders of Hogwarts.

Harry, Ron, and Hermione go hunting for these Horcruxes so they can destroy them. During the Battle of Hogwarts, the last of the Horcruxes is destroyed, and Harry is finally able to defeat Voldemort once and for all. That's game over, Voldy!

BELLATRIX LESTRANGE

Bellatrix Lestrange is one of Lord Voldemort's most loyal (and dangerous) followers. Bellatrix spends fifteen years in Azkaban Prison for hurting two Aurors (Dark wizard catchers) with the Cruciatus Curse. Eventually, she escapes Azkaban Prison during a mass breakout. C'mon, Dementors, you had *one* job to do!

While many people in her family also support Lord Voldemort (like her sister, Narcissa and nephew, Draco), others are just the opposite. Bellatrix is related to Sirius Black and Nymphadora Tonks, who are dedicated members of an organization that fights Voldemort. That's gotta make the holidays a bit awkward!

Bellatrix gets in big trouble with Voldemort when Harry, Ron, and Hermione escape her clutches after they are caught hunting for Horcruxes. The three friends even use Polyjuice Potion to impersonate Bellatrix and break into her personal Gringotts vault! But Bellatrix returns to fight at the Battle of Hogwarts.

FUN FACT: BELLATRIX AND SIRIUS BLACK ARE COUSINS.

I'M VOLDEMORT'S FAVORITE. HE'S NEVER TOLD ME THAT EXACTLY, BUT I KNOW HE'S THINKING IT.

HOGWARTS HOUSE: SLYTHERIN

EPIC MOMENT: WHEN BELLATRIX DUELS WITH SIRIUS!

Lucius and Narcissa Malfoy are the parents of Harry's nemesis, Draco, and supporters of Lord Voldemort. Lucius manages to avoid punishment after Voldemort's first downfall by being all, "Volde-who?" when the Ministry of Magic questions him. But when Voldemort comes back, Lucius immediately returns to his side.

Some families may have their own farm passed down through generations, some may have a family restaurant—the Malfoys have Voldemort. Draco joins his followers in his sixth year, and Malfoy Manor becomes Voldemort's headquarters. But Narcissa isn't quite as loyal as the rest of her family. She thinks it's too dangerous for her son to be involved with the Dark Lord.

During the chaos at the Battle of Hogwarts, Lucius and Narcissa don't know if Draco is safe. Narcissa lies to Voldemort (and helps Harry in the process) so that she can go to the castle and find her son. After they reunite, the Malfoy family decides that they'd rather be together than risk their lives for Voldemort, and they leave the battle. Good villain servants are *so* hard to find these days!

PETER PETTIGREW

Peter Pettigrew attended Hogwarts alongside Sirius Black, Remus Lupin, and Harry's father, James Potter. Together, the four friends called themselves the Marauders. But Peter eventually betrays them to become one of Voldemort's followers. He tells Voldemort where the Potters are hiding with their baby son, Harry. Then he frames Sirius Black for giving away the secret and goes into hiding.

Everyone thinks Peter died a hero, but really, he turns into a rat! (How appropriate.) Peter is an Animagus, and he pretends to be the Weasleys' pet rat, Scabbers, for twelve years. When Sirius escapes from Azkaban Prison, Peter is finally forced to reveal his true self. Some might say he was better as a rat!

He soon escapes capture again and returns to Voldemort's side, helping his master return to power. Bet you he really missed Mrs. Weasley's delicious cooking!

I'M CRAVING SOME CHEESE.
ANIMAGUS: RAT
ALSO KNOWN AS: "WORMTAIL" AND "SCABBERS"

ORDER
OF THE

THE ORDER OF THE PHOENIX IS AN ORGANIZATION OF WITCHES AND WIZARDS WHO JOIN FORCES TO FIGHT VOLDEMORT AND HIS FOLLOWERS.

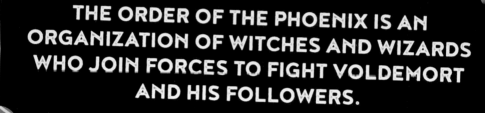

THEIR HEADQUARTERS IS LOCATED AT NUMBER TWELVE, GRIMMAULD PLACE, AN ENCHANTED BUILDING THAT APPEARS ONLY FOR THOSE WHO HAVE BEEN NOTIFIED OF ITS SECRET LOCATION.

IF ONLY YOU COULD PUT THAT CHARM ON YOUR BEDROOM DOOR WHEN YOU WANT SOME PRIVACY!

PHOENIX

FOR AN ENTIRE YEAR, ALMOST NOBODY BELIEVES HARRY POTTER'S STORY ABOUT VOLDEMORT RISING TO POWER ONCE AGAIN—BUT THE MEMBERS OF THE ORDER OF THE PHOENIX KNOW IT'S THE TRUTH.

THE ORDER HAS SPIES WITHIN THE MINISTRY OF MAGIC TO FIND OUT VOLDEMORT'S PLANS. THEY ALSO DO WHATEVER THEY CAN TO PROTECT HARRY—EVEN WHEN HE TRIES TO THROW HIMSELF IN THE MIDDLE OF THE ACTION (WHICH IS OFTEN).

SIRIUS BLACK
TWELVE YEARS FLY BY WHEN YOU'RE PLOTTING REVENGE!
ALSO KNOWN AS: "PADFOOT" AND "SNUFFLES"

Sirius Black is a member of the Order of the Phoenix and godfather to Harry Potter. Sirius is one of the four Marauders along with James Potter, Peter Pettigrew, and Remus Lupin.

After the Potters are attacked by Voldemort, everyone thinks Sirius betrayed them. Really, Peter framed Sirius, sending him to Azkaban Prison for twelve years. Then Sirius escapes! He goes to Hogwarts in his Animagus form to find Peter and get revenge.

When Sirius finally reveals himself, he tells Harry, Ron, Hermione, and his old friend Lupin the truth about what happened. But then Peter gets away and Sirius is captured! Harry and Hermione help Sirius escape the Dementors, but he is forced to go on the run again. It's all siriusly dramatic!

ANIMAGUS: BLACK DOG

SIRIUS
BLACK

Sirius offers his abandoned childhood home, number 12, Grimmauld Place, to be the new headquarters for the Order of the Phoenix. This lets Sirius stay involved in the Order even though he can't leave the house for fear of going back to Azkaban Prison.

Sirius hates being cooped up all the time and not being able to help Harry when he's in trouble. They send each other letters and even communicate using Floo powder, which allows Sirius's head to appear in the fireplace of the Gryffindor common room. Way cooler than video chat! (Though, admittedly, more dangerous.)

In Harry's fifth year, Voldemort tricks Harry into thinking that his godfather is in trouble. Harry runs off to the Department of Mysteries to rescue him before realizing it's a trap. Luckily, members of the Order, including Sirius, come to fight Voldemort's followers. But during the battle, Sirius is pushed through a mysterious veil by his cousin, Bellatrix Lestrange, never to be seen again.

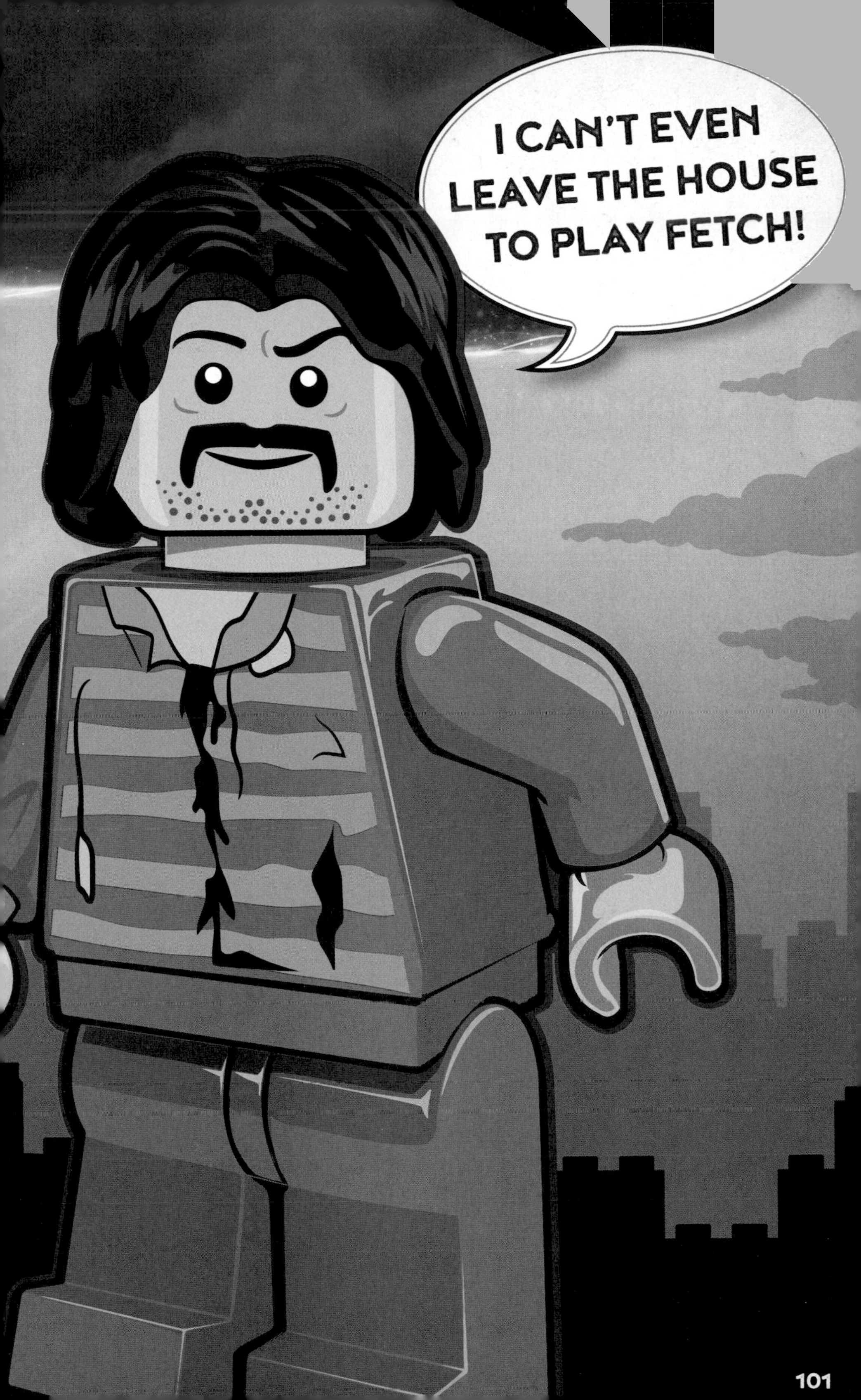
I CAN'T EVEN LEAVE THE HOUSE TO PLAY FETCH!

NYMPHADORA TONKS

Nymphadora Tonks (known just as "Tonks" if you know what's good for you) is a Metamorphmagus, which means she can change her appearance at will. This ability comes in handy during her work catching Dark wizards as an Auror—and also when she wants to amuse her friends at the dinner table.

Tonks's job in the Order is to help protect Harry. She is also in charge of protecting a Fake Potter right before Harry's seventeenth birthday. Six of Harry's friends transform themselves to look like him using Polyjuice Potion. That way, Voldemort's followers don't know which Harry is the real one. Sneaky!

Tonks marries Remus Lupin. They have a son, Teddy, whom they leave behind when they go to fight at the Battle of Hogwarts.

PINK HAIR, DON'T CARE!

FUN FACT:
TONKS USES HER METAMORPHMAGUS ABILITIES TO GIVE HERSELF PINK HAIR.

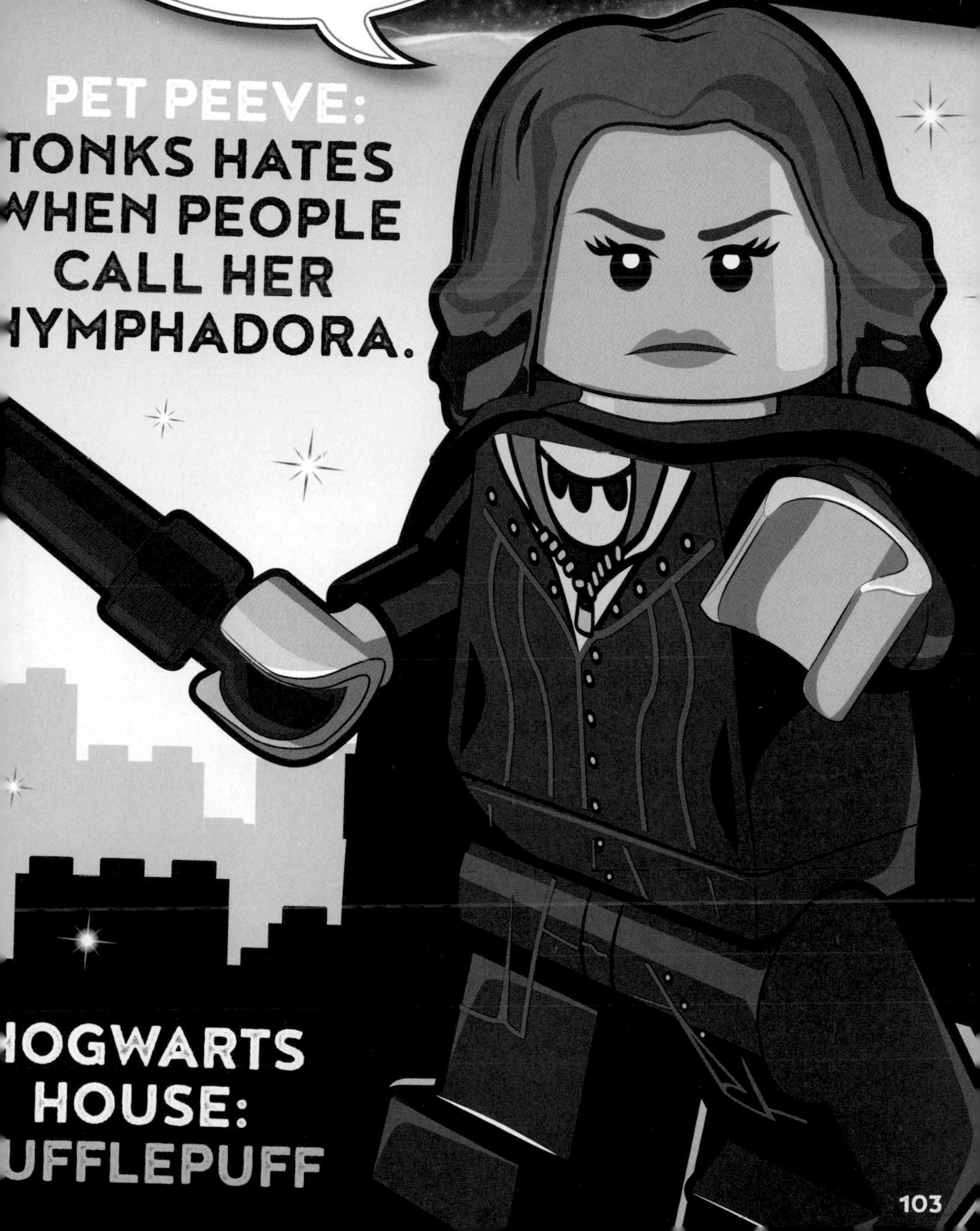

PET PEEVE:
TONKS HATES WHEN PEOPLE CALL HER NYMPHADORA.

HOGWARTS HOUSE:
HUFFLEPUFF

REAL NAME: ALASTOR MOODY

Mad-Eye Moody is an Auror best known for his scary—uh, *intense*—personality and unique appearance. He suffered many injuries during his years of hunting Dark wizards for the Ministry of Magic. His career teaches him to be suspicious of everything. Never offer him a goblet of pumpkin juice, no matter how delicious it is—he just may hex you for trying to poison him!

Mad-Eye gets his nickname for his left eye. This fake eye is magic and often spins around in the eye socket on its own. It can see through anything, from wood to invisibility cloaks. This makes it a great tool for an Auror—and for a teacher, like when Moody can spot students sticking gum to the bottom of their desks.

Well, technically the teacher isn't actually Moody. He's supposed to work as the Defense Against the Dark Arts professor at Hogwarts during Harry's fourth year. Instead, one of Voldemort's followers kidnaps Moody, steals his magic eye, and takes his place using Polyjuice Potion that makes him look exactly like Moody. No wonder the poor guy is so paranoid!

FUN FACT: IN ADDITION TO A MAGICAL EYE, MOODY HAS A WOODEN LEG.

MOLLY WEASLEY

Molly Weasley is the head of the Weasley family. She is a stay-at-home mother and never stops working for her seven children. She keeps track of where each family member is at any moment thanks to a magical clock that points to locations instead of numbers. Yet somehow Fred and George still manage to get away with plenty of mischief!

Molly treats Harry and Hermione like her own children. She's always happy to welcome more people into her home during summer vacations and holidays. And when Molly knits sweaters for her family for Christmas, she always makes some for Harry. Who cares if they're a bit lumpy? It's the thought that counts!

Molly keeps things running smoothly at the Order of the Phoenix headquarters. She doesn't want her younger kids or Harry and Hermione getting involved in dangerous Order business. But they all end up fighting together at the Battle of Hogwarts, where Molly defeats Bellatrix Lestrange in an epic duel!

EVERYONE IS WELCOME AT THE BURROW—EXCEPT FRED AND GEORGE WHEN THEY'VE JUST GOT ANOTHER DETENTION.

FUN FACT: THE WEASLEYS' HOUSE IS CALLED THE BURROW.

FAVORITE SINGER:

CELESTINA WARBECK

Arthur Weasley is the father of the seven Weasley children and Molly's husband. He is the less serious parent, and Molly often has to remind him to discipline the kids when they've done something wrong.

Arthur works in the Misuse of Muggle Artefacts Office at the Ministry of Magic. He investigates whenever a Muggle encounters a magical object. Arthur is endlessly fascinated by Muggles and the devices they use to get by without magic. If he saw you using a cell phone, he would probably faint from excitement!

Like the rest of his family, Arthur is a member of the Order of the Phoenix. In Harry's fifth year, Harry has a vision of Arthur being attacked by a snake during a top secret Order mission. Arthur is injured, but Harry's vision gets him help in time to save his life.

HOGWARTS HOUSE:
GRYFFINDOR, LIKE ALL THE WEASLEYS!

KINGSLEY
SHACKLEBOLT

Kingsley is an Auror at the Ministry of Magic alongside Tonks and Mad-Eye Moody. He accompanies them as part of Harry's protective detail when Harry is not at Hogwarts. Kingsley spies within the Ministry to gather information for the Order of the Phoenix in their fight against You-Know-Who.

Kingsley fights in the battle at the Department of Mysteries, and he is an important player in the plan to move Harry to safety before his seventeenth birthday. Kingsley is assigned to protect Hermione, who is disguised as one of the Fake Potters, and the pair of them are attacked by Voldemort himself! Luckily, both Kingsley and Hermione know a thing or two about fighting bad guys.

During Bill Weasley's wedding, Kingsley sends his Patronus to the middle of the dance floor—but not to get down and boogie! His Patronus warns everyone that Voldemort has taken over the Ministry of Magic and his supporters are on their way, giving the wedding guests a chance to escape.

PATRONUS: LYNX

JOB:

AURORA FOR THE MINISTRY OF MAGIC

FUN FACT:

KINGSLEY IS APPOINTED MINISTER FOR MAGIC AFTER THE BATTLE OF HOGWARTS.

CONCLUSION

From Hogwarts founders to Hogwarts students, from Dark wizards to the wizards who bravely sta... up to them: now you know all about some of the most fascinating people in the Wizarding World.

But you've only just scratched the surface of what this magical world has in store. Besides witches and wizards, there are goblins, house elves, Merpeople, and more. There's even someone more unusual than Luna Lovegood: her dad!

Even with all the fantastic creatures and peculia... people, there will always be one wizard who stands out among all of it: the Boy Who Lived.